Easy Air Fryer Cookbook 2021

A Beginner's Guide To Enjoy Your Delicious Air Fryer Dishes to Help Lose Weight and Live Healthier

Megan Miller

Disclaimer Notice:

Table Of Content

Introduction

Congratulations on purchasing your copy of *Easy Air Fryer Cookbook 2021: A Beginner's Guide To Enjoy Your Delicious Air Fryer Dishes to Help Lose Weight and Live Healthier,* and thank you for doing so.

I'm glad that you have chosen to take this opportunity to welcome the **Air Fryer Diet** into your life. I'm sure this book will help you find all the information and tools you need to better integrate the **Air Fryer Diet** plan with your habits.

Also, I thought I would share with you some delicious ideas and recipes for all tastes and for the best of your low carb diet, which I hope you will appreciate.

You will find hundreds of easy to realize ideas that will best suit your situation or your needs at the moment, with all the preparation time, amount of servings, and the list of all the nutritional values you'll need.

BREAKFAST

Egg Whites with Sliced Tomatoes

Preparation time: 10 minutes • Cooking time: 15 minutes •
Servings: 2

INGREDIENTS

- 1 tomato, sliced
- 2 egg whites
- ¼ teaspoon ground paprika
- ¼ teaspoon salt
- 1 teaspoon olive oil
- 1 teaspoon dried dill

DIRECTIONS

1. Pour the olive oil in the air fryer.
2. Then add the egg whites.
3. Sprinkle the egg whites with the salt, dried dill, and ground paprika.
4. Cook the egg whites for 15 minutes at 350 F.
5. When the egg whites are cooked – let them chill little.
6. Place the layer of the sliced tomatoes on the plate.
7. Then chop the egg whites roughly and place over the tomatoes.
8. Serve!

NUTRITION: Calories 45, Fat 2.5, Fiber 0.5, Carbs 1.9, Protein 4

Eggs in Avocado

Preparation time: 10 minutes • Cooking time: 7 minutes •
Servings: 2

INGREDIENTS

- 1 avocado, pitted
- 2 eggs
- ½ ground black pepper
- ¾ teaspoon salt

DIRECTIONS

1. Cut the avocado into the halves.
2. Then sprinkle the avocado with the black pepper and salt.
3. Beat the eggs and place them in the avocado halve's wholes.
4. Place the avocado in the air fryer basket.
5. Cook the meal for 7 minutes at 380 F.
6. When the eggs are cooked – the meal is ready to eat.
7. Serve it immediately!

NUTRITION: Calories 268, Fat 24, Fiber 6.7, Carbs 9, Protein 7.5

Whisked Eggs with Ground Chicken

Preparation time: 10 minutes • Cooking time: 15 minutes •
Servings: 4

INGREDIENTS

- 3 eggs, whisked
- 1 cup ground chicken
- ½ teaspoon salt
- 1 oz fresh parsley, chopped
- ½ teaspoon ground paprika
- ½ onion, chopped

DIRECTIONS

1. Put the ground chicken in the air fryer basket.
2. Add salt, chopped parsley, and ground paprika.
3. After this, add the chopped onion and stir the mixture with the help of the wooden spatula.
4. Cook the ground chicken mixture for 8 minutes at 375 F.
5. Stir it time to time.
6. Then pour the whisked eggs over the ground chicken mixture and cook it for 7 minutes more at 365 F.

7. When the meal is cooked – stir it carefully and transfer in the serving bowls.
8. Serve it immediately!

NUTRITION: Calories 122, Fat 6.6, Fiber 0.6, Carbs 2.1, Protein 14.7

Kale Quiche with Eggs

Preparation time: 10 minutes • Cooking time: 18 minutes •
Servings: 6

INGREDIENTS

- 1 cup kale
- 3 eggs
- 2 oz bacon, chopped, cooked
- 1 sweet potato, grated
- ½ teaspoon thyme
- ½ teaspoon ground black pepper
- ½ teaspoon ground paprika
- ½ cup coconut milk
- 1 onion, chopped
- 1 teaspoon olive oil

DIRECTIONS

1. Chop the kale roughly and place it in the blender.
2. Blend it gently.
3. Then transfer the blended kale in the mixing bowl.
4. Add the grated potato and thyme.
5. Sprinkle the mixture with the ground black pepper and ground paprika.
6. Add coconut milk and chopped onion.
7. Pour the olive oil into the air fryer basket.
8. Then place the kale mixture in the air fryer basket,

9. Beat the eggs in the separate bowl and whisk well.

10. Pour the whisked eggs over the kale mixture. Add bacon.

11. Cook the quiche for 18 minutes at 350 F.

12. When the time is over – chill the quiche little and serve!

NUTRITION: Calories 166, Fat 11.8, Fiber 1.8, Carbs 8.5, Protein 7.7

Spinach Frittata

Preparation time: 15 minutes •Cooking time: 15 minutes • Servings: 4

INGREDIENTS

- 4 eggs, beaten
- 1 cup spinach
- 1 tablespoon almond flour
- 1 teaspoon coconut flour
- 1/3 teaspoon ground paprika
- 1 teaspoon basil, dried
- ½ teaspoon salt
- 1 teaspoon olive oil

DIRECTIONS

1. Whisk the eggs.
2. Then place the spinach in the blender and blend well.
3. Add the spinach in the whisked eggs.
4. After this, add the almond flour and coconut flour.
5. Sprinkle the mixture with the ground paprika.
6. Add dried basil and salt.

7. Stir the mixture.

8. Pour the olive oil in the frittata molds.

9. Then add the frittata mixture and transfer the molds in the air fryer basket.

10. Cook the frittata for 15 minutes at 350 F.

11. Chill the cooked frittata to the room temperature and serve!

NUTRITION: Calories 118, Fat 9.2, Fiber 1.2, Carbs 2.6, Protein 7.4

Beef Balls with Sesame and Dill

Preparation time: 10 minutes • Cooking time: 10 minutes •
Servings: 4

INGREDIENTS

- 1 teaspoon sesame seeds
- 1 tablespoon dill, dried
- 1 egg
- 10 oz ground beef
- 1 garlic clove, chopped
- ¾ teaspoon nutmeg
- 1 teaspoon olive oil
- 1 teaspoon almond flour

DIRECTIONS

1. Beat the egg in the bowl and whisk it.
2. Add dried dill and sesame seeds.
3. Stir gently and add chopped garlic clove and nutmeg.
4. Then add ground beef and almond flour.
5. Mix the mixture carefully with the help of the spoon.
6. Pour the olive oil in the air fryer basket.
7. Make the medium balls from the meat mixture and place them in the air fryer.
8. Cook the meatballs for 10 minutes at 380 F.
9. Stir the meatballs during the cooking with

the help of the wooden spatula.

10. Transfer the cooked meatballs in the serving bowls.

11. Enjoy!

NUTRITION: Calories 207, Fat 10.7, Fiber 1.1, Carbs 2.7, Protein 24.7

MAIN

Thai Roast Beef Salad with Nam Jim Dressing

Cooking Time: 30 minutes Servings: 2

INGREDIENTS

- ½ lb. fresh beef without bone
- Sea salt and pepper to taste
- 1teaspoon olive oil
- For Beef Dressing:
- 2tablespoons of fresh lime juice
- 2tablespoons of fish sauce
- A piece of ginger about 1-inch long
- 2garlic cloves
- 2tablespoons sesame oil
- 2tablespoons Tamari sauce
- 4tablespoons pure water
- Pinch of salt
- To Prepare Salad:
- 1carrot, diced
- 1small white cabbage, chopped
- 1red pepper, sliced
- 2teaspoons toasted sesame seeds
- ½ cup coriander leaves, chopped
- 2teaspoons bean sprouts, chopped
- Half a dozen sugar snap peas, finely sliced

DIRECTIONS

1. Set the air fryer to 375° Fahrenheit and cook beef for 30-minutes. Mix oil, salt, and pepper with roast beef. Cook at 300° Fahrenheit for an additional 10- minutes. Mix all the ingredients for the salad and set aside. Add all the salad ingredients into food processor and blend for 2- minutes to thin dressing. Allow the roast beef to cool down for about 20- minutes. Cut the beef into wafer thin slices. Garnish with coriander, lime wedges, and toasted sesame seeds. Mound salad on a dish then top with meat slices.

NUTRITION: Calories: 312, Total Fat: 11.6g, Carbs: 9.2g, Protein: 38.2g

Stuffed Garlic Chicken

Cooking Time: 15 minutes • Servings: 2

INGREDIENTS

- ¼ cup of tomatoes, sliced
- ½ tablespoon garlic, minced
- 2basil leaves
- Salsa for serving
- 1prosciutto slice
- 2teaspoons parmesan cheese, freshly grated
- 2boneless chicken breasts
- Pepper and salt to taste

DIRECTIONS

1. Cut the side of the chicken breast to make a pocket. Stuff each pocket with tomato slices, garlic, grated cheese and basil leaves. Cut a slice of prosciutto in half to form 2 equal size pieces. Season chicken with salt and pepper and wrap each with a slice of prosciutto. Preheat your air fryer to 325°Fahrenheit. Place the stuffed chicken breasts into air fryer basket and cook for 15-minutes. Serve chicken breasts with salsa.

Rosemary Citrus Chicken

Cooking Time: 15 minutes • Servings: 2

INGREDIENTS

- 1lb. chicken thighs
- 1/2 teaspoon rosemary, fresh, chopped
- 1/8 teaspoon thyme, dried
- ½ cup tangerine juice
- 2tablespoons white wine
- 1teaspoon garlic, minced
- Salt and pepper to taste
- 2tablespoons lemon juice

DIRECTIONS

1. Place the chicken thighs in a mixing bowl. In another bowl, mix tangerine juice, garlic, white wine, lemon juice, rosemary, pepper, salt, and thyme. Pour the mixture over chicken thighs and place in the fridge for 20-minutes. Preheat your air fryer to 350°Fahrenheit and place your marinated chicken in air fryer basket and cook for 15-minutes. Serve hot and enjoy!

NUTRITION: Calories: 473, Total Fat: 17g, Carbs: 7g, Protein: 66g

Air Fried Chicken Thighs

Cooking Time: 12 minutes Servings: 2

INGREDIENTS

- 2boneless chicken thighs
- Salt and pepper to taste
- 1teaspoon rosemary, dried
- 1tablespoon Worcestershire sauce
- 1tablespoon oyster sauce
- 1teaspoon liquid stevia
- 2garlic cloves, minced

DIRECTIONS

1. Add ingredients to a bowl and combine well. Place the marinated chicken in the fridge for an hour. Preheat your air fryer to 180°Fahrenheit for 3-minutes. Add marinated chicken to air fryer grill pan and cook for 12-minutes. Serve hot!

NUTRITION: Calories: 270, Total Fat: 17g, Carbs: 7g, Protein: 20g

Stuffed Turkey

Cooking Time: 63 minutes • Servings: 6

INGREDIENTS

- 1whole turkey, bone-in, with skin
- 2celery stalks, chopped
- 1lemon, sliced
- Fresh oregano leaves, chopped
- 1cup fresh parsley, minced
- 1teaspoon sage leaves, dry
- 2cups turkey broth
- 4cloves garlic, minced
- 1onion, chopped
- 2eggs
- 1½ lbs sage sausage
- 4tablespoons butter

DIRECTIONS

1. Preheat your air fryer to 390°Fahrenheit. In a pan over medium- heat melt 2 ½ tablespoons of butter. Add the sausage (remove sausage meat from skinand mash. Cook sausage meat in the pan for 8-minutes and stir. Add in celery, onions, garlic, and sage and cook for an additional 10-minutes, stir to combine. Remove sausage mixture from heat and add the broth. In a bowl, whisk eggs and two tablespoons of parsley.

Pour egg mixture into sausage mix and stir. This will be the stuffing for your turkey. Fill the turkey with the stuffing mix. In a separate bowl, combine the remaining butter with parsley, oregano, salt, and pepper and rub this mix onto turkey skin. Place the turkey inside the air fryer and cook for 45- minutes. Garnish with lemon slices.

NUTRITION: Calories: 1046, Total Fat: 69.7g, Carbs: 12.7g, Protein: 91.5g

SIDES

Collard Greens Sauté

Preparation Time: 20 minutes

Servings: 4

Ingredients:

- 1 lb. collard greens

- 2 tbsp. chicken stock

- 1 tbsp. balsamic vinegar

- ¼ cup cherry tomatoes; halved

- A pinch of salt and black pepper

Directions:

1. In a pan that fits your air fryer, mix the collard greens with the other ingredients, toss gently, introduce in the air fryer and cook at 360°F for 15 minutes

2. Divide between plates and serve as a side dish.

Nutrition: Calories: 121; Fat: 3g; Fiber: 4g; Carbs: 6g; Protein: 5g

Roasted Garlic

Preparation Time: 25 minutes

Servings: 12 cloves

Ingredients:

- 1 medium head garlic

- 2 tsp. avocado oil

Directions:

1. Remove any hanging excess peel from the garlic but leave the cloves covered. Cut off ¼ of the head of garlic, exposing the tips of the cloves

2. Drizzle with avocado oil. Place the garlic head into a small sheet of aluminum foil, completely enclosing it. Place it into the air fryer basket. Adjust the temperature to 400 Degrees F and set the timer for 20 minutes. If your garlic head is a bit smaller, check it after 15 minutes

3. When done, garlic should be golden brown and very soft

4. To serve, cloves should pop out and easily be spread or sliced. Store in an airtight container in the refrigerator up to 5 days.

5. You may also freeze individual cloves on a baking sheet, then store together in a freezer-safe storage bag once frozen.

Nutrition: Calories: 11; Protein: 0.2g; Fiber: 0.1g; Fat: 0.7g; Carbs: 1.0g

Roasted Veggies

Preparation Time: 25 minutes

Servings: 4

Ingredients:

- 1 lb. Brussels sprouts; halved

- 8 oz. brown mushrooms; halved

- 8 oz. cherry tomatoes; halved

- 1 tbsp. olive oil

- 1 tsp. rosemary; dried

- Juice of 1 lime

- A pinch of salt and black pepper

Directions:

Take a bowl and mix all the ingredients, toss, put them in your air fryer's basket, cook at 380°F for 20 minutes, divide between plates and serve as a side dish

Nutrition: Calories: 163; Fat: 4g; Fiber: 2g; Carbs: 4g; Protein: 8g

Spinach and Artichokes Sauté

Preparation Time: 20 minutes

Servings: 4

Ingredients:

- 10 oz. artichoke hearts; halved

- 2 cups baby spinach

- 3 garlic cloves

- ¼ cup veggie stock

- 2 tsp. lime juice

- Salt and black pepper to taste.

Directions:

1. In a pan that fits your air fryer, mix all the ingredients, toss, introduce in the fryer and cook at 370°F for 15 minutes

2. Divide between plates and serve as a side dish.

Nutrition: Calories: 209; Fat: 6g; Fiber: 2g; Carbs: 4g; Protein: 8g

Roasted Carrot Strips

Preparation Time: 10 minutes

Cooking time: 10 minutes

Servings: 2

Ingredients:

- 2 carrots

- 1 teaspoon brown sugar

- 1 teaspoon olive oil

- 1 tablespoon soy sauce

- 1 teaspoon honey

- ½ teaspoon ground black pepper

Directions:

1. Peel the carrot and cut it into the strips.

2. Then put the carrot strips in the bowl.

3. Sprinkle the carrot strips with the olive oil, soy sauce, honey, and ground black pepper.

4. Shake the mixture gently.

5. Preheat the air fryer to 360 F.

6. Cook the carrot for 10 minutes.

7. After this, shake the carrot strips well.

8. Enjoy!

Nutrition: calories 67, fat 2.4, fiber 1.7, carbs 11.3, protein 1.1

Green Bean Casserole

Preparation Time: 25 minutes

Servings: 4

Ingredients:

- 1 lb. fresh green beans, edges trimmed

- ½ oz. pork rinds, finely ground

- 1 oz. full-fat cream cheese

- ½ cup heavy whipping cream.

- ¼ cup diced yellow onion

- ½ cup chopped white mushrooms

- ½ cup chicken broth

- 4 tbsp. unsalted butter.

- ¼ tsp. xanthan gum

Directions:

1. In a medium skillet over medium heat, melt the butter. Sauté the onion and mushrooms until they become soft and fragrant, about 3–5 minutes.

2. Add the heavy whipping cream, cream cheese and broth to the pan. Whisk until smooth. Bring to a boil and then reduce to a simmer. Sprinkle the xanthan gum into the pan and remove from heat

3. Chop the green beans into 2-inch pieces and place into a 4-cup round baking dish. Pour the sauce mixture over them and stir until coated. Top the dish with ground

pork rinds. Place into the air fryer basket

4. Adjust the temperature to 320 Degrees F and set the timer for 15 minutes. Top will be golden and green beans fork tender when fully cooked. Serve warm.

Nutrition: Calories: 267; Protein: 3.6g; Fiber: 3.2g; Fat: 23.4g; Carbs: 9.7g

Turkey Breast with Maple Mustard Glaze

Cooking Time: 42 minutes • Servings: 6

INGREDIENTS

- 5lbs. of boneless turkey breast
- ¼ Maple Syrup sugar-free
- 2tablespoons Dijon Mustard
- 1tablespoon butter
- 2olive oil
- Dried herbs: sage, thyme, smoked paprika
- Salt and pepper to taste

DIRECTIONS

1. Preheat air fryer to 350°Fahrenheit. Rub turkey breasts with olive oil. Combine the spices and season the turkey on the outside with this mix of spices. Place the turkey in air fryer and cook for 25- minutes. Turn over and cook for an additional 12-minutes more. In a small saucepan over medium heat mix the maple syrup, mustard, and butter. Brush the turkey with the glaze in an upright position. Air fry for 5-minutes or until turkey breasts is golden in color.

NUTRITION: Calories: 464, Total Fat: 10g, Carbs: 25g, Protein: 64.6g

SEAFOOD

Baked Snapper

Preparation time: 10 minutes • Cooking time: 15 minutes •
Servings: 4

INGREDIENTS

- 1pound snapper fillets, boneless
- 1tablespoon lemon juice
- 1tablespoon olive oil
- ½ teaspoon cumin, ground
- Salt and black pepper to the taste

DIRECTIONS

1. In the air fryer's basket, mix the snapper with the lemon juice and the other ingredients, cook at 380 degrees F for 15 minutes, divide everything between plates and serve with a side salad.

NUTRITION: Calories 191, Fat 2, Fiber 3, Carbs 18, Protein 12

Trout and Red Chili Mix

Preparation time: 10 minutes • Cooking time: 15 minutes •
Servings: 4

INGREDIENTS

- 4trout fillets, boneless
- Salt and black pepper to the taste
- 1red chili pepper, chopped
- 1green chili pepper, chopped
- 1cup heavy cream
- 1tablespoon lemon juice

DIRECTIONS

1. In the air fryer's pan, mix the fish with the chilies
   and the other ingredients, toss, cook at 360
   degrees F for 15 minutes, divide between plates
   and serve.

NUTRITION: Calories 271, Fat 4, Fiber 2, Carbs 15,
Protein 11

Scallops Mix

Preparation time: 10 minutes • Cooking time: 15 minutes
•Servings: 4

INGREDIENTS

- 1pound scallops
- 1red bell pepper, chopped
- ½ cup white wine
- ½ teaspoon sweet paprika
- Salt and black pepper to the taste
- A drizzle of olive oil

DIRECTIONS

1. In the air fryer's pan, mix the scallops with the wine and the other ingredients and cook at 380 degrees F and cook for 15 minutes, stirring halfway.
2. Divide between plates and serve.

NUTRITION: Calories 290, Fat 12, Fiber 2, Carbs 16, Protein 19

Shrimp and Cucumber Mix

Preparation time: 5 minutes • Cooking time: 10 minutes • Servings: 4

INGREDIENTS

- 1pound shrimp, deveined and peeled
- 1cup cucumber, roughly cubed
- 1tablespoon avocado oil
- 1tablespoon balsamic vinegar
- ½ cup coconut cream
- 1tablespoon parsley, chopped
- Salt and black pepper to the taste

DIRECTIONS

1. In a pan that fits your air fryer, mix the shrimp with the cucumber and the other ingredients, toss, introduce in the fryer and cook at 360 degrees F for 10 minutes.
2. Divide into bowls and serve.

NUTRITION: Calories 272, Fat 4, Fiber 3, Carbs 14, Protein 4

Shrimp Scampi Linguine

Preparation Time: 25 minutes

Servings: 4

Nutrition: 560 Calories; 15.1g Fat; 47.3g Carbs; 59.3g Protein; 1.6g Sugars

Ingredients

- 1 ½ pounds shrimp, shelled and deveined

- 1/2 tablespoon fresh basil leaves, chopped

- 2 tablespoons olive oil

- 2 cloves garlic, minced

- 1/2 teaspoon fresh ginger, grated

- 1/4 teaspoon cracked black pepper

- 1/2 teaspoon sea salt

- 1/4 cup chicken stock

- 2 ripe tomatoes, pureed

- 8 ounces linguine pasta

- 1/2 cup parmesan cheese, preferably freshly grated

Directions

1. Start by preheating the Air Fryer to 395 degrees F. Place the shrimp, basil, olive oil, garlic, ginger, black pepper, salt, chicken stock, and tomatoes in the casserole dish.

2. Transfer the casserole dish to the cooking basket and bake for 10 minutes.

3. Bring a large pot of lightly salted water to a boil. Cook the linguine for 10 minutes or until al dente; drain.

4. Divide between four serving plates. Add the shrimp sauce and top with parmesan cheese. Bon appétit!

Sunday Fish with Sticky Sauce

Preparation Time: 20 minutes

Servings: 2

Nutrition: 573 Calories; 38.3g Fat; 31.5g Carbs; 26.2g Protein; 5.7g Sugars

Ingredients

- 2 pollack fillets

- Salt and black pepper, to taste

- 1 tablespoon olive oil

- 1 cup chicken broth

- 2 tablespoons light soy sauce

- 1 tablespoon brown sugar

- 2 tablespoons butter, melted

- 1 teaspoon fresh ginger, minced

- 1 teaspoon fresh garlic, minced

- 2 corn tortillas

Directions

1. Pat dry the pollack fillets and season them with salt and black pepper; drizzle the sesame oil all over the fish fillets.

2. Preheat the Air Fryer to 380 degrees F and cook your fish for 11 minutes. Slice into bite-sized pieces.

3. Meanwhile, prepare the sauce. Add the broth to a large saucepan and bring to a boil. Add the soy sauce, sugar, butter, ginger, and garlic. Reduce the heat to simmer and cook until it is reduced slightly.

4. Add the fish pieces to the warm sauce. Serve on corn tortillas and enjoy!

POULTRY

Parmesan Chicken

Preparation time: 10 minutes • Cooking time: 30 minutes •
Servings: 4

INGREDIENTS:

- 2pounds chicken breast, skinless, boneless and cubed
- 1cup parmesan, grated
- ¼ cup butter, melted
- 1teaspoon garam masala
- Salt and black pepper to the taste
- 1tablespoon chives, chopped

DIRECTIONS

1. In the air fryer's pan, mix the chicken with the parmesan and the other ingredients, cook at 380 degrees F for 30 minutes, divide between plates and serve.

NUTRITION: Calories 271, Fat 9, Fiber 4, Carbs 19, Protein 15

Chicken, Sweet Potatoes and Radishes

Preparation time: 10 minutes • Cooking time: 30 minutes •
Servings: 4

INGREDIENTS

- 1pound chicken breast, skinless, boneless and cubed
- 1cup radishes, halved
- 2sweet potatoes, peeled and cubed
- 2tablespoons olive oil
- 1teaspoon turmeric powder
- Salt and black pepper to the taste
- 1tablespoon parsley, chopped

DIRECTIONS

1. In the air fryer's pan, mix the chicken with the radishes and the other ingredients, toss and cook at 360 degrees F for 30 minutes.
2. Divide everything between plates and serve.

NUTRITION: Calories 290, Fat 13, Fiber 4, Carbs 10, Protein 16

Chicken with Apples and Dates

Preparation time: 10 minutes • Cooking time: 25 minutes •
Servings: 4

INGREDIENTS

- 2pounds chicken breast skinless, boneless and cubed
- 1cup apples, cored and cubed
- 1cup dates
- 1/3 cup white wine
- salt and black pepper to the taste
- 1tablespoon avocado oil

DIRECTIONS

1. In the air fryer's pan, mix the chicken with the apples and the other ingredients, and cook at 370 degrees F for 25 minutes.
2. Divide the mix between plates and serve.

NUTRITION: Calories 270, Fat 14, Fiber 3, Carbs 15, Protein 20

Chicken with Carrots and Celery

Preparation time: 10 minutes • Cooking time: 30 minutes • Servings: 4

INGREDIENTS

- 2pounds chicken breast, skinless, boneless and cubed
- 1cup carrots, peeled and sliced
- 1cup celery, chopped
- 1tablespoon avocado oil
- 1tablespoon balsamic vinegar
- Salt and black pepper to the taste
- 2tablespoon chives, chopped

DIRECTIONS

1. In the air fryer's pan, mix the chicken with the carrots and the other ingredients, put it in your air fryer and cook at 350 degrees F for 30 minutes.
2. Divide the mix between plates and serve.

NUTRITION: Calories 237, Fat 10, Fiber 4, Carbs 19, Protein 16

Chicken with Cauliflower Rice

Preparation time: 10 minutes • Cooking time: 30 minutes •
Servings: 4

INGREDIENTS

- 1cup cauliflower rice
- 1cup chicken stock
- 2pounds chicken thighs, boneless, skinless and cubed
- ¼ cup tomato sauce
- 3garlic cloves, minced
- Salt and black pepper to the taste
- 1tablespoon olive oil
- 1tablespoon parsley, chopped

DIRECTIONS

1. In a pan that fits your air fryer, mix the chicken with the cauliflower rice and the other ingredients, introduce the pan in the fryer, cook at 370 degrees F for 30 minutes, divide between plates and serve.

NUTRITION: Calories 280, Fat 12, Fiber 12, Carbs 16, Protein 13

Chicken and Pineapple Mix

Preparation time: 10 minutes • Cooking time: 25 minutes •
Servings: 4

INGREDIENTS

- 2pounds chicken breast, skinless, boneless and cubed
- 1cup pineapple, peeled and cubed
- 2tablespoons avocado oil
- 1tablespoon rosemary, chopped
- Salt and black pepper to the taste
- ½ teaspoon chili powder
- 2tablespoons honey

DIRECTIONS

1. In the air fryer's pan, mix the chicken with the pineapple and the other ingredients, toss, cook at 390 degrees F for 25 minutes, divide between plates and serve.

NUTRITION: Calories 281, Fat 11, Fiber 12, Carbs 28, Protein 19

MEAT

Shallot and Celery Steak

Preparation Time: 17 minutes

Servings: 6

Nutrition: 368 Calories; 13.3g Fat; 8.3g Carbs; 50.1g Protein; 0.6g Sugars; 0.8g Fiber

Ingredients

- 1/3 cup cream of shallot soup

- 2 sprigs fresh rosemary, chopped

- 1 cup celery, sliced

- 1/2 cup tomatoes, crushed

- 2 sprigs fresh thyme, chopped

- 1 teaspoon kosher salt

- 4 tablespoons dry white wine

- 1 teaspoon ground black pepper, or to taste

- 6 lean steaks, cut into strips

- 3 shallots, peeled and cut into wedges

- 1/2 teaspoon cayenne pepper

Directions

1. Add all ingredients to an Air Fryer baking tray; then, cook for 13 minutes at 395 degrees F.

2. Work in batches; pause the machine once or twice to shake your food. Bon appétit!

Tender and Creamy Beef with Sage

Preparation Time: 13 minutes

Servings: 2

Nutrition: 428 Calories; 20.1g Fat; 6.7g Carbs; 50.1g Protein; 0.9g Sugars; 1.3g Fiber

Ingredients

- 1/3 cup sour cream

- ½ cup green onion, chopped

- 1 tablespoon mayonnaise

- 3 cloves garlic, smashed

- 1 pound beef flank steak, trimmed and cubed

- 2 tablespoons fresh sage, minced

- ½ teaspoon salt

- 1/3 teaspoon black pepper, or to taste

Directions

1. Season your meat with salt and pepper; arrange beef cubes on the bottom of a baking dish that fits in your air fryer.

2. Stir in green onions and garlic; air-fry for about 7 minutes at 385 degrees F.

3. Once your beef starts to tender, add the cream, mayonnaise, and sage; air-fry an additional 8 minutes. Bon appétit!

Ginger Turkey and Yogurt mix

Preparation time: 10 minutes • Cooking time: 25 minutes • Servings: 4

INGREDIENTS

- 2pounds turkey breast, skinless, boneless and cubed
- 1cup Greek yogurt
- 2tablespoons ginger, grated
- Salt and black pepper to the taste
- 1teaspoon chili powder
- 2teaspoons olive oil
- 1tablespoon cilantro, chopped

DIRECTIONS

1. In the air fryer's pan, mix the turkey with the yogurt and the other ingredients, toss and cook at 400 degrees F for 25 minutes
2. Divide everything between plates and serve.

NUTRITION: Calories 245, Fat 4, Fiber 5, Carbs 17, Protein 16

Moroccan Beef Kebab

Preparation Time: 30 minutes

Servings: 4

Nutrition: 354 Calories; 15.5g Fat; 6g Carbs; 49g Protein; 2.6g Sugars; 1.6g Fiber

Ingredients

- 1/2 cup leeks, chopped

- 2 garlic cloves, smashed

- 2 pounds ground chuck

- Salt, to taste

- 1/4 teaspoon ground black pepper, or more to taste

- 1 teaspoon cayenne pepper

- 1/2 teaspoon ground sumac

- 3 saffron threads

- 2 tablespoons loosely packed fresh continental parsley leaves

- 4 tablespoons tahini sauce

- 4 ounces baby arugula

- 1 tomato, cut into slices

Directions

1. In a bowl, mix the chopped leeks, garlic, ground chuck, and spices; knead with your hands until everything is well incorporated.

2. Now, mound the beef mixture around a wooden skewer into a pointed-ended sausage.

3. Cook in the preheated Air Fryer at 360 degrees F for 25 minutes.

4. Serve your kebab with the tahini sauce baby arugula and tomato. Enjoy!

Thai Curried Meatballs

Preparation Time: 20 minutes

Servings: 4

Nutrition: 242 Calories; 10.5g Fat; 0.2g Carbs; 34.4g Protein; 0g Sugars; 0.4g Fiber

Ingredients

- 1 pound ground beef

- 1 teaspoon red Thai curry paste

- 1/2 lime, rind and juice

- 1 teaspoon Thai seasoning blend

- 2 teaspoons lemongrass, finely chopped

- 1 tablespoon sesame oil

Directions

1. Thoroughly combine all ingredients in a mixing dish.

2. Shape into 24 meatballs and place them into the Air Fryer cooking basket. Cook at 380 degrees F for 10 minutes; pause the machine and cook for a further 5 minutes, or until cooked through.

3. Serve accompanied by the dipping sauce. Bon appétit!

Pesto Chicken Wings

Preparation time: 10 minutes • Cooking time: 35 minutes • Servings: 4

INGREDIENTS

- 2pounds chicken wings
- 3tablespoons basil pesto
- Salt and black pepper to the taste
- ¼ cup butter, melted
- 4garlic cloves, minced
- 1teaspoon turmeric powder

DIRECTIONS

1. In the fryer's basket, mix the chicken wings with the pesto and the other ingredients, rub well and at 400 degrees F for 35 minutes.
2. Divide the chicken between plates, and serve.

NUTRITION: Calories 274, Fat 11, Fiber 3, Carbs 19, Protein 15

Italian Peperonata with a Twist

Preparation Time: 35 minutes

Servings: 4

Nutrition: 563 Calories; 41.5g Fat; 10.6g Carbs; 35.6g Protein; 7.9g Sugars; 1g Fiber

Ingredients

- 2 teaspoons canola oil

- 2 bell peppers, sliced

- 1 green bell pepper, sliced

- 1 serrano pepper, sliced

- 1 shallot, sliced

- Sea salt and pepper, to taste

- 1/2 dried thyme

- 1 teaspoon dried rosemary

- 1/2 teaspoon mustard seeds

- 1 teaspoon fennel seeds

- 2 pounds thin beef parboiled sausage

Directions

1. Brush the sides and bottom of the cooking basket with 1 teaspoon of canola oil. Add the peppers and shallot to the cooking basket.

2. Toss them with the spices and cook at 390 degrees F for 15 minutes, shaking the basket occasionally. Reserve.

3. Turn the temperature to 380 degrees F

4. Then, add the remaining 1 teaspoon of oil. Once hot, add the sausage and cook in the preheated Air Frye for 15 minutes, flipping them halfway through the cooking time.

5. Serve with reserved pepper mixture. Bon appétit!

Buttery Tender New York Strip

Preparation Time: 20 minutes

Servings: 4

Nutrition: 439 Calories; 27.4g Fat; 1.3g Carbs; 48.3g Protein; 0.6g Sugars; 0.3g Fiber

Ingredients

- 1 tablespoon peanut oil

- □ 2 pounds New York Strip

- 1 teaspoon cayenne pepper

- Sea salt and freshly cracked black pepper, to taste

- 1/2 stick butter, softened

- 1 teaspoon whole-grain mustard

Directions

1. Rub the peanut oil all over the steak; season with cayenne pepper, salt, and black pepper.

2. Cook in the preheated Air Fryer at 400 degrees F for 7 minutes; turn over and cook an additional 7 minutes.

3. Meanwhile, prepare the mustard butter by whisking the butter, whole-grain mustard, and honey.

4. Serve the roasted New York Strip dolloped with the mustard butter. Bon appétit!

EGGS AND DAIRY

Stuffed Mushrooms with Cheese

Preparation Time: 15 minutes

Servings: 5

Nutrition: 188 Calories; 15.7g Fat; 4.4g Carbs; 8.4g Protein; 1.6g Sugars; 0.8g Fiber

Ingredients

- 1/2 cup parmesan cheese, grated

- 2 cloves garlic, pressed

- 2 tablespoons fresh coriander, chopped

- 1/3 teaspoon kosher salt

- ☐ 1/2 teaspoon crushed red pepper flakes

- 1 ½ tablespoons olive oil

- 20 medium-sized mushrooms, cut off the stems

- 1/2 cup Gorgonzola cheese, grated

- 1/4 cup low-fat mayonnaise

- 1 teaspoon prepared horseradish, well-drained

- 1 tablespoon fresh parsley, finely chopped

Directions

1. Mix the parmesan cheese together with the garlic, coriander, salt, red pepper, and the olive oil; mix to combine well.

2. Stuff the mushroom caps with the parmesan filling. Top with grated Gorgonzola.

3. Place the mushrooms in the Air Fryer grill pan and slide them into the machine. Grill them at 380 degrees F for 8 to 12 minutes or until the stuffing is warmed through.

4. Meanwhile, prepare the horseradish mayo by mixing the mayonnaise, horseradish and parsley. Serve with the warm fried mushrooms. Enjoy!

VEGETABLES

Veggies Stuffed Eggplants

Preparation Time: 20 minutes

Cooking time: 14 minutes

Servings: 5

Ingredients:

- 10 small eggplants, halved lengthwise

- 1 onion, chopped

- 1 tomato, chopped

- ¼ cup cottage cheese, chopped

- ½ green bell pepper, seeded and chopped

- 1 tablespoon fresh lime juice

- 1 tablespoon vegetable oil

- ½ teaspoon garlic, chopped

- Salt and ground black pepper, as required

- 2 tablespoons tomato paste

Directions:

1. Preheat the Air fryer to 320 0 F and grease an Air fryer basket.

2. Cut a slice from one side of each eggplant lengthwise and scoop out the flesh in a bowl.

3. Drizzle the eggplants with lime juice and arrange in the Air fryer basket.

4. Cook for about 4 minutes and remove from the Air fryer.

5. Heat vegetable oil in a skillet over medium heat and add garlic and onion.

6. Sauté for about 2 minutes and stir in the eggplant flesh, tomato, salt, and black pepper.

7. Sauté for about 3 minutes and add cheese, bell pepper, tomato paste, and cilantro.

8. Cook for about 1 minute and stuff this mixture into the eggplants.

9. Close each eggplant with its cut part and set the Air fryer to 360 0 F.

10. Arrange in the Air fryer basket and cook for about 5 minutes.

11. Dish out in a serving plate and serve hot.

Nutrition:

Calories: 83, Fat: 3.2g, Carbohydrates: 11.9g, Sugar: 6.1g, Protein: 3.4g, Sodium: 87mg

Buttered Broccoli

Preparation Time: 10 minutes

Cooking time: 7 minutes

Servings: 4

Ingredients:

- 4 cups fresh broccoli florets

- 2 tablespoons butter, melted

- ¼ cup water

- Salt and black pepper, to taste

Directions:

1. Preheat the Air fryer to 400 0 F and grease an Air fryer basket.

2. Mix broccoli, butter, salt, and black pepper in a bowl and toss to coat well.

3. Place water at the bottom of Air fryer pan and arrange the broccoli florets into the Air fryer basket.

4. Cook for about 7 minutes and dish out in a bowl to serve hot.

Nutrition:

Calories: 82, Fat: 6.1g, Carbohydrates: 6g, Sugar: 1.6g, Protein: 2.6g, Sodium: 110mg

Rice and Beans Stuffed Bell Peppers

Preparation Time: 15 minutes

Cooking time: 15 minutes

Servings: 5

Ingredients:

- 1, 15-ouncescan diced tomatoes with juice

- 1, 15-ouncescan red kidney beans, rinsed and drained

- 1 cup cooked rice

- 5 large bell peppers, tops removed and seeded

- ½ cup mozzarella cheese, shredded

- 1½ teaspoons Italian seasoning

Directions:

1. Preheat the Air fryer to 360 o F and grease an Air fryer pan.

2. Mix rice, tomatoes with juice, beans, and Italian seasoning in a bowl.

3. Stuff the rice mixture in each bell pepper half and arrange in the Air fryer pan.

4. Cook for about 12 minutes and top with mozzarella cheese.

5. Cook for about 3 more minutes and dish out to serve warm.

Nutrition: Calories: 487, Fat: 2.5g, Carbohydrates: 94.3g, Sugar: 10.2g, Protein: 24.6g, Sodium: 37mg

Caramelized Carrots

Preparation Time: 10 minutes

Cooking time: 15 minutes

Servings: 3

Ingredients:

- 1 small bag baby carrots

- ½ cup butter, melted

- ½ cup brown sugar

Directions:

1. Preheat the Air fryer to 400 0 F and grease an Air fryer basket.

2. Mix the butter and brown sugar in a bowl.

3. Add the carrots and toss to coat well.

4. Arrange the carrots in the Air fryer basket and cook for about 15 minutes.

5. Dish out and serve warm.

Nutrition:

Calories: 416, Fat: 30.9g, Carbohydrates: 36.2g, Sugar: 30.7g, Protein: 1.3g, Sodium: 343mg

SNACKS

Meatballs with Mediterranean Dipping Sauce

Cooking Time: 15 minutes • Servings: 4

INGREDIENTS

- For the meatballs:
- 1½ tablespoons melted butter
- 2eggs
- ½ tablespoon red pepper flakes, crushed
- 2tablespoons fresh mint leaves, finely chopped
- 4garlic cloves, finely minced
- ½ lb. ground pork
- 2tablespoons capers
- For the Mediterranean dipping sauce:
- 1/3 cup black olives, pitted, chopped finely
- 2tablespoons fresh rosemary
- ½ teaspoon dill, dried
- 1/3 cup Greek yogurt
- ½ teaspoon lemon zest
- 2tablespoons parsley

DIRECTIONS

1. Start the preheating of your air-fryer at 395°Fahrenheit. In a large bowl, add meatball ingredients and combine well. Shape into golf ball size balls. Cook the meatballs for about 9- minutes. Meanwhile, prepare your dipping sauce, by whisking all the ingredients. Serve meatballs warm with Mediterranean sauce.

NUTRITION: Calories: 52, Total Fat: 2.32g, Carbs: 3.04g, Protein: 7.45g

Mayo-Cheddar Jacket Potatoes

Cooking Time: 10 minutes • Servings: 8

INGREDIENTS

- 1/3 cup cheddar cheese, grated
- 3tablespoons mayonnaise
- Sea salt, ground black pepper and cayenne pepper to taste
- 2tablespoons chives, chopped
- 1½ tablespoons olive oil
- 8Russet potatoes
- ½ cup soft cheese, softened

DIRECTIONS

1. Stab potatoes with a fork. Preheat your air-fryer to 360°Fahrenheit. Bake the potatoes for 10-minutes in the air-fryer basket. Meanwhile, prepare your filling by mixing the rest of the above ingredients. Stuff potatoes with the prepared filling. Serve immediately!

NUTRITION: Calories: 327, Total Fat: 7g, Carbs: 59g, Protein: 9.4g

Air-Fried Roasted Potatoes with Rosemary

Cooking Time: 30 minutes • Servings: 4

INGREDIENTS

- 2cups potatoes, diced
- 2teaspoons rosemary, dried
- 1teaspoon sesame oil
- 1teaspoon black pepper

DIRECTIONS

1.   Preheat your air-fryer to 370°Fahrenheit. Add potatoes and spray them with sesame oil. Heat for 30-minutes and shake air-fryer basket a couple of times during cook time. Garnish with rosemary and serve warm.

NUTRITION: Calories: 203, Total Fat: 9.53g, Carbs: 27.28g, Protein: 3.11g

Potato Fries with Bean Sprouts & Peanut Herb Salad

Cooking Time: 20 minutes • Servings: 4

INGREDIENTS

- 2cups potato (cut into strips
- ¾ cup bean sprouts
- 2tablespoons parsley leaves, chopped
- 2tablespoons basil leaves, chopped
- 1teaspoon, pepper
- 1teaspoon salt
- 1tablespoon Sriracha sauce
- ½ cup roasted peanuts
- 1tablespoon rice vinegar
- 2teaspoons olive oil

DIRECTIONS

1. Preheat your air-fryer to 390°Fahrenheit and then place potato fries into the air- fryer basket. Spray a teaspoon of olive oil and season with salt. Cook for 15- minutes and shake basket a few times during cook time. After potato fries are cooked, save them for later use.

2. Prepare half a cup of peanuts. Preheat your air-fryer to 400°Fahrenheit and put half a cup of peanuts in the basket. Spray a teaspoon of olive

oil and cook for 5- minutes. Once roasted, set aside.

3. Now, get a large mixing bowl, combine bean sprouts, chopped parsley, basil leaves in a bowl. Add the potato fries and roasted into a bowl. Season with Sriracha sauce and rice vinegar. Sprinkle with pepper. Toss and serve right away.

NUTRITION: Calories: 163, Total Fat:0.7g, Carbs: 34.2g, Protein: 5.03g

Sweet & Spicy Tofu with Steamed Spinach

Cooking Time: 24 minutes • Servings: 6

INGREDIENTS

- 6cups of spinach, chopped
- 2teaspoons rice vinegar
- 1teaspoon agave syrup
- 1teaspoon salt
- 2-inches ginger, minced
- 1teaspoon sesame oil
- 1tablespoon vegan oyster sauce
- 1teaspoon red pepper flakes
- 1lb. tofu cubed

DIRECTIONS

1. Rinse and drain the tofu. Make sure to press the tofu to remove excess water. Cut tofu into small cubes and place them in a mixing bowl. Add minced ginger to bowl with tofu. Add agave syrup, season with salt, red pepper flakes and stir. Let mixture stand for 30- minutes before frying.

2. Prepare spinach by steaming for 4- minutes, then transfer spinach to bowl. Add vegan oyster sauce and rice vinegar and toss and save for later use. Preheat air-fryer to 370°Fahrenheit. Add the marinated tofu and spray with a teaspoon of

sesame oil. Cook for 20-minutes and shake the air-fryer basket every 5-minutes during cook time. Once cooked, transfer the tofu to bowl with steamed spinach mix. Toss all ingredients and serve warm.

NUTRITION: Calories: 169, Total Fat: 10.8g, Carbs: 6.8g, Protein: 15.2g

Air-Fried Walnuts & Green Beans

Cooking Time: 20 minutes • Servings: 5

INGREDIENTS

- ½ teaspoon chili powder
- 4cups green beans, cut into 3-inch long pieces
- ¼ cup walnuts, roasted
- 4garlic cloves, chopped
- 1tablespoon light soy sauce
- 1teaspoon sugar-free maple syrup
- 1teaspoon sesame oil
- Salt and pepper to taste

DIRECTIONS

1. After washing and chopping vegetable place into a bowl. Prepare by using a mortar and pestle, pound walnuts lightly and then transfer to a bowl of vegetables. Add remaining ingredients to a bowl, except sesame oil. Preheat your air-fryer to 390°Fahrenheit. Add marinated beans and walnuts to air-fryer and spray them with sesame oil. Cook for 20-minutes and shake the basket a couple of times during the cook time. Serve warm.

NUTRITION: Calories: 155, Total Fat: 12.41g, Carbs: 9.18g, Protein: 4.68g

DESSERT

Chocolate Chips Cream

Preparation time: 10 minutes • Cooking time: 15 minutes • Servings: 4

INGREDIENTS

- 1cup coconut cream
- 2tablespoons sugar
- 1tablespoon cocoa powder
- 1teaspoon cinnamon powder
- 1cup heavy cream
- 1cup chocolate chips

DIRECTIONS:

1. In a bowl, mix the cream with the sugar and the other ingredients, whisk and divide into 4 ramekins.
2. Put the ramekins in the air fryer, cook at 340 degrees F for 15 minutes and serve cold.

NUTRITION: Calories 190, Fat 2, Fiber 1, Carbs 6, Protein 3

Cinnamon Cream

Preparation time: 10 minutes • Cooking time: 20 minutes • Servings: 4

INGREDIENTS:

- 1cup cream cheese, soft
- 1cup coconut cream
- ½ cup heavy cream
- 3tablespoons sugar
- 1and ½ tablespoons cinnamon powder
- 2eggs, whisked

DIRECTIONS

1. In the air fryer's pan, combine the cream cheese with the cream and the other ingredients, whisk well, cook at 350 degrees F for 20 minutes, divide into bowls and serve warm.

NUTRITION: Calories 200, Fat 11, Fiber 2, Carbs 15, Protein 4

Pumpkin Bowls

Preparation time: 10 minutes • Cooking time: 15 minutes •
Servings: 4

INGREDIENTS

- 2cups pumpkin flesh, cubed
- 1cup heavy cream
- 1teaspoon cinnamon powder
- 3tablespoons sugar
- 1teaspoon nutmeg, ground

DIRECTIONS

1. In a pan that fits your air fryer, combine the pumpkin with the cream and the other ingredients, introduce in the fryer and cook at 360 degrees F for 15 minutes.
2. Divide into bowls and serve.

NUTRITION: Calories 212, Fat 5, Fiber 2, Carbs 15, Protein 7

Mango and Pears Bowls

Preparation time: 10 minutes • Cooking time: 15 minutes • Servings: 4

INGREDIENTS

- 2pears, cored and cut into wedges
- 1cup mango , peeled and roughly cubed
- 1cup apple juice
- 1teaspoon nutmeg, ground
- ½ teaspoon cinnamon powder
- 2tablespoons sugar

DIRECTIONS

1. In the air fryer's pan, mix the pears with the mango and the other ingredients, put the pan in the machine and cook at 320 degrees F for 15 minutes.
2. Divide into bowls and serve warm.

NUTRITION: Calories 210, Fat 2, Fiber 1, Carbs 12, Protein 3

Orange Bread with Almonds

Preparation time: 20 minutes • Cooking time: 40 minutes • Servings: 8

INGREDIENTS

- 1orange, peeled and sliced
- Juice of 2 oranges
- 3tablespoons vegetable oil
- 2tablespoons flax meal combined with 2 tablespoons water
- ¾ cup coconut sugar+ 2 tablespoons
- ¾ cup whole wheat flour
- ¾ cup almonds, ground

DIRECTIONS

1. Grease a loaf pan with some oil, sprinkle 2 tablespoons sugar and arrange orange slices on the bottom.
2. In a bowl, mix the oil with ¾ cup sugar, almonds, flour and orange juice, stir, spoon this over orange slices, place the pan in your air fryer and cook at 360 degrees F for 40 minutes.
3. Slice and serve the bread right away.
4. Enjoy!

NUTRITION: Calories 202, Fat 3, Fiber 2, Carbs 6, Protein 6

Tangerine Cake

Preparation time: 10 minutes • Cooking time: 20 minutes • Servings: 8

INGREDIENTS:

- ¾ cup coconut sugar
- 2cups whole wheat flour
- ¼ cup olive oil
- ½ cup almond milk
- 1teaspoon cider vinegar
- ½ teaspoon vanilla extract
- Juice and zest of 2 lemons
- Juice and zest of 1 tangerine

DIRECTIONS

1. In a bowl, mix flour with sugar and stir.
2. In another bowl, mix oil with milk, vinegar, vanilla extract, lemon juice and zest, tangerine zest and flour, whisk very well, pour this into a cake pan that fits your air fryer, introduce in the fryer and cook at 360 degrees F for 20 minutes.
3. Serve right away.
4. Enjoy!

NUTRITION: Calories 210, Fat 1, Fiber 1, Carbs 6, Protein 4

Carrot and Zucchini Cake

Preparation time: 10 minutes • Cooking time: 40 minutes • Servings: 6

INGREDIENTS

- 1and ½ cups almond flour
- ½ cup carrots, peeled and grated
- ½ cup zucchinis, grated
- ½ teaspoon baking soda
- 2eggs, whisked
- 3tablespoons butter, melted
- 3tablespoons sugar
- ½ cup coconut cream
- Cooking spray

DIRECTIONS

1. In a bowl, mix the flour with the zucchinis, carrots and the other ingredients except the cooking spray and whisk well.
2. Pour this into a cake pan that fits your air fryer greased with cooking spray, transfer to your air fryer, cook at 320 degrees F for 40 minutes, cool down, cut and serve it.

NUTRITION: Calories 200, Fat 6, Fiber 7, Carbs 12, Protein 4

Apples Cheesecake

Preparation time:10 minutes • Cooking time: 25 minutes • Servings: 6

INGREDIENTS

- 2tablespoons butter, melted
- 1cup graham cookies, crumbled
- 1cup apples, cored and cubed
- 1cup cream cheese, soft
- 2tablespoon sugar
- ½ teaspoon almond extract
- ½ teaspoon vanilla extract

DIRECTIONS

1. In a bowl, mix the melted butter with the graham cookies, stir and press on the bottom of a cake pan that fits the air fryer.
2. In a bowl, mix the rest of the ingredients, whisk, spread over the cookie crust, introduce in your air fryer and cook at 340 degrees F for 25 minutes.
3. Serve the cheesecake really cold.

NUTRITION: Calories 212, Fat 12, Fiber 6, Carbs 12, Protein 7

Maple Tomato Bread

Preparation time: 10 minutes • Cooking time: 30 minutes •
Servings: 4

INGREDIENTS

- 1and ½ cups whole wheat flour
- 1teaspoon cinnamon powder
- 1teaspoon baking powder
- 1teaspoon baking soda
- ¾ cup maple syrup
- 1cup tomatoes, chopped
- ½ cup olive oil
- 2tablespoon apple cider vinegar

DIRECTIONS

1. In a bowl, mix flour with baking powder, baking soda, cinnamon and maple syrup and stir well.
2. In another bowl, mix tomatoes with olive oil and vinegar and stir well.
3. Combine the 2 mixtures, stir well, pour into a greased loaf pan that fits your air fryer, introduce in the fryer and cook at 360 degrees F for 30 minutes.
4. Leave the cake to cool down, slice and serve.
5. Enjoy!

NUTRITION: Calories 203, Fat 2, Fiber 1, Carbs 12, Protein 4

Lemon Squares

Preparation time: 10 minutes • Cooking time: 30 minutes •
Servings: 6

INGREDIENTS

- 1cup whole wheat flour
- ½ cup vegetable oil
- 1and ¼ cups coconut sugar
- 1medium banana
- 2teaspoons lemon peel, grated
- 2tablespoons lemon juice
- 2tablespoons flax meal combined with 2 tablespoons water
- ½ teaspoon baking powder

DIRECTIONS:

1. In a bowl, mix flour with ¼ cup sugar and oil, stir well, press on the bottom of a pan that fits your air fryer, introduce in the fryer and bake at 350 degrees F for 14 minutes.
2. In another bowl, mix the rest of the sugar with lemon juice, lemon peel, banana, and baking powder, stir using your mixer and spread over baked crust.
3. Bake for 15 minutes more, leave aside to cool down, cut into medium squares and serve cold.

4. Enjoy!

NUTRITION: Calories 140, Fat 4, Fiber 1, Carbs 12, Protein 1

Peach Cinnamon Cobbler

Preparation time: 10 minutes • Cooking time: 30 minutes • Servings: 4

INGREDIENTS

- 4cups peaches, peeled and sliced
- ¼ cup coconut sugar
- ½ teaspoon cinnamon powder
- 1and ½ cups vegan crackers, crushed
- ¼ cup stevia
- ¼ teaspoon nutmeg, ground
- ½ cup almond milk
- 1teaspoon vanilla extract
- Cooking spray

DIRECTIONS

1. In a bowl, mix peaches with coconut sugar and cinnamon and stir.
2. In a separate bowl, mix crackers with stevia, nutmeg, almond milk and vanilla extract and stir.

3. Spray a pie pan that fits your air fryer with cooking spray and spread peaches on the bottom.

4. Add crackers mix, spread, introduce into the fryer and cook at 350 degrees F for 30 minutes

5. Divide the cobbler between plates and serve.

6. Enjoy!

NUTRITION: Calories 201, Fat 4, Fiber 4, Carbs 7, Protein 3

Easy Pears Dessert

Preparation time: 10 minutes • Cooking time: 25 minutes •
Servings: 12

INGREDIENTS

- 6big pears, cored and chopped
- ½ cup raisins
- 1teaspoon ginger powder
- ¼ cup coconut sugar
- 1teaspoon lemon zest, grated

DIRECTIONS

1. In a pan that fits your air fryer, mix pears with raisins, ginger, sugar and lemon zest, stir, introduce in the fryer and cook at 350 degrees F for 25 minutes.
2. Divide into bowls and serve cold.
3. Enjoy!

NUTRITION: Calories 200, Fat 3, Fiber 4, Carbs 6, Protein 6

Coconut Pancake

Preparation time: 10 minutes • Cooking time: 40 minutes • Servings: 4

INGREDIENTS

- 2cups self-raising flour
- 2tablespoons sugar
- 2eggs
- 1and ½ cups coconut milk
- A drizzle of olive oil

DIRECTIONS

1. In a bowl, mix eggs with sugar, milk and flour and whisk until you obtain a batter.
2. Grease your pressure cooker with the oil, add the batter, spread into the pot, cover and cook on Low for 40 minutes.
3. Slice pancake, divide between plates and serve cold.

NUTRITION: Calories 162, Fat 3, Fiber 2, Carbs 7, Protein

Apples and Red Grape Juice

Preparation time: 10 minutes • Cooking time: 10 minutes • Servings: 2

INGREDIENTS

- 2apples
- ½ cup natural red grape juice
- 2tablespoons raisins
- 1teaspoon cinnamon powder
- ½ tablespoons sugar

DIRECTIONS:

1. Put the apples in your pressure cooker, add grape juice, raisins, cinnamon and stevia, toss a bit, cover and cook on High for 10 minutes.
2. Divide into 2 bowls and serve.

NUTRITION: Calories 110, Fat 1, Fiber 1, Carbs 3, Protein

Strawberry Shortcakes

Preparation time: 20 minutes • Cooking time: 25 minutes • Servings: 2

INGREDIENTS

- Cooking spray
- 3tablespoons sugar
- 1cup white flour
- 1cup water
- ½ teaspoon baking powder
- ¼ teaspoon baking soda
- 3tablespoons butter
- ½ cup buttermilk
- 1egg, whisked
- 1and ½ tablespoons sugar
- 1cups strawberries, sliced
- ½ tablespoon rum
- ½ tablespoon mint, chopped
- ½ teaspoon lime zest, grated

DIRECTIONS

1. In a bowl, mix flour with 2 tablespoons sugar, baking powder and baking soda and stir.
2. In another bowl, mix buttermilk with egg, stir, add to flour mixture and whisk

everything.

3. Spoon this dough into 2 jars greased with cooking spray and cover with tin foil.

4. Add the water to your pressure cooker, add the steamer basket inside, add jars, cover cooker and cook on High for 25 minutes.

5. Meanwhile, in a bowl, mix strawberries with 1 tablespoon sugar, rum, mint and lime zest and toss to coat

6. Divide strawberry mix on shortcakes and serve.

Coconut and Avocado Pudding

Preparation time: 2 hours • Cooking time: 2 minutes •
Servings: 3

INGREDIENTS

- ½ cup avocado oil
- 4tablespoons sugar
- 1tablespoon cocoa powder
- 14ounces canned coconut milk
- 1avocado,   pitted,   peeled   and chopped

DIRECTIONS

1. In a bowl, mix oil with cocoa powder and half of the sugar, stir well, transfer to a lined container, keep in the fridge for 1 hour and chop into small pieces.

2. In your pressure cooker, mix coconut milk with avocado and the rest of the sugar, blend using an immersion blender, cover cooker and cook on High for 2 minutes.

3. Add chocolate chips, stir, divide pudding into bowls and keep in the fridge until you serve it.

NUTRITION: Calories 140, Fat 3, Fiber 2, Carbs 3, Protein

Cocoa and Milk Pudding

Preparation time: 50 minutes • Cooking time: 3 minutes • Servings: 4

INGREDIENTS

- 1and ½ cups water, for the pressure cooker+ 2 tablespoons
- 2tablespoons gelatin
- 4tablespoons sugar
- 4tablespoons cocoa powder
- 2cups coconut milk, hot
- ½ teaspoon cinnamon powder

DIRECTIONS

1. In a bowl, mix milk with sugar, cinnamon and cocoa powder and stir well.
2. In a bowl, mix gelatin with 2 tablespoons water, stir well, add to cocoa mix, stir and divide into ramekins.
3. Add the water to your pressure cooker, add the steamer basket, add ramekins inside, cover and cook on High for 4 minutes.
4. Serve puddings cold.

NUTRITION: Calories 120, Fat 2, Fiber 1, Carbs 4, Protein

Conclusion

Thank you for making it through to the end of ***Easy Air Fryer Cookbook 2021: A Beginner's Guide To Enjoy Your Delicious Air Fryer Dishes to Help Lose Weight and Live Healthier***, let's hope it was informative and able to provide you with all of the tools you need to achieve your goals whatever they may be.

The **Air Fryer** may take some time to get accustomed to. It takes time to determine new habits and become familiar with food replacement methods, including how to make low-cost food tasty and satisfying.

But if you keep up with it, it can become a replacement way of life that is natural and budget-friendly. It can also lead to some important health improvements, especially if you are suffering from any condition, keto diet proves to be helpful. And better health can mean fewer doctor visits and lower medical costs.

Finally, if you found this book useful in any way, a review is always appreciated!